DATE DUE

B
Lab   Orr, Tamra
       Shia LaBeouf

North Valley Middle School

$19.00

AR
RL
5.9
PTS
1

139943 Shia LaBeouf

Shia
LaBEOUF

Tamra Orr

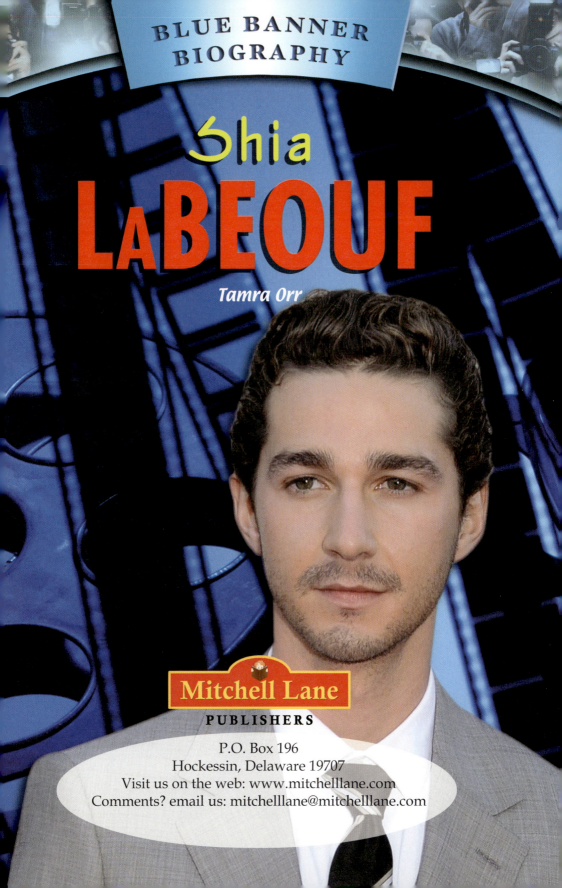

Mitchell Lane
PUBLISHERS

P.O. Box 196
Hockessin, Delaware 19707
Visit us on the web: www.mitchelllane.com
Comments? email us: mitchelllane@mitchelllane.com

Mitchell Lane
PUBLISHERS

Printing   1   2   3   4   5   6   7   8   9

Blue Banner Biographies

Akon	Flo Rida	Megan Fox
Alicia Keys	Gwen Stefani	Miguel Tejada
Allen Iverson	Ice Cube	Missy Elliott
Ashanti	Ja Rule	Nancy Pelosi
Ashlee Simpson	Jamie Foxx	Natasha Bedingfield
Ashton Kutcher	Jay-Z	Orianthi
Avril Lavigne	Jennifer Lopez	Orlando Bloom
Beyoncé	Jessica Simpson	P. Diddy
Blake Lively	J. K. Rowling	Peyton Manning
Bow Wow	Joe Flacco	Pink
Brett Favre	John Legend	Queen Latifah
Britney Spears	Johnny Depp	Rihanna
Carrie Underwood	Justin Berfield	Robert Pattinson
Chris Brown	Justin Timberlake	Ron Howard
Chris Daughtry	Kanye West	Sean Kingston
Christina Aguilera	Kate Hudson	Selena
Christopher Paul Curtis	Keith Urban	Shakira
Ciara	Kelly Clarkson	Shia LaBeouf
Clay Aiken	Kenny Chesney	Shontelle Layne
Cole Hamels	Kristen Stewart	Soulja Boy Tell 'Em
Condoleezza Rice	Lady Gaga	Stephenie Meyer
Corbin Bleu	Lance Armstrong	Taylor Swift
Daniel Radcliffe	Leona Lewis	T.I.
David Ortiz	Lil Wayne	Timbaland
David Wright	Lindsay Lohan	Tim McGraw
Derek Jeter	Mariah Carey	Toby Keith
Drew Brees	Mario	Usher
Eminem	Mary J. Blige	Vanessa Anne Hudgens
Eve	Mary-Kate and Ashley Olsen	Zac Efron
Fergie		

Library of Congress Cataloging-in-Publication Data
Orr, Tamra.
 Shia LaBeouf / by Tamra Orr.
   p. cm. — (Blue banner biographies)
 Includes bibliographical references and index.
 Includes filmography and webliography.
 ISBN 978-1-58415-908-7 (library bound)
 1. LaBeouf, Shia, 1986– —Juvenile literature. 2. Actors—United States—Biography—Juvenile literature. I. Title.
 PN2287.L12O66 2010
 791.4302′8092—dc22
 [B]
                                                                        2010008947

ABOUT THE AUTHOR: Tamra Orr is the author of more than 250 books for young people and families, including Mitchell Lane's biographies on Jordin Sparks, Brenda Song, and Orlando Bloom. A former English teacher, she lives in the Pacific Northwest, where she alternates between her research and looking at the mountains. Orr's books have won several national awards.

PUBLISHER'S NOTE: The following story has been thoroughly researched, and to the best of our knowledge represents a true story. While every possible effort has been made to ensure accuracy, the publisher will not assume liability for damages caused by inaccuracies in the data and makes no warranty on the accuracy of the information contained herein. This story has not been authorized or endorsed by Shia LaBeouf.

Father and son share a moment in the spotlight at the 2005 Toronto Film Festival. Although the two of them move in different circles, they have built a strong relationship over the years.

The Snow Cone
Family Circus

The Snow Cone Family Circus definitely caught people's attention as it paraded down the Los Angeles sidewalk. The family was white—which already made them noticeable in this mainly Latino neighborhood. Second, Dad was very tall, Mom was quite short, and their two-year-old son was just adorable. Finally, all three were dressed as clowns and trying to sell as many hot dogs and snow cones as possible before the end of the day.

Popular actor Shia LaBeouf (pronounced SHY-uh luh-BUFF), the toddler from that family, remembers the experience quite well. "We were the only white family around, so we figured we could do the look-at-us thing and dance around like a bunch of idiots," he told a reporter from *Time* magazine. "I hated selling hot dogs. I hated dressing up as a clown. But the minute somebody would buy into my thing and buy a hot dog from my family because of my shtick, my parents would look at me like, 'All right, man.' Besides performing, I've never had that validation from anything else I've ever done in my life."

A proud mother poses with her son at the 2003 premiere of The Battle of Shaker Heights. *Shia and his mother have been close all of his life.*

The thrill of performing—or, in this case, selling hot dogs—and the appreciation of his first audience (his parents) would stay with Shia for the rest of his life. It would also help him discover his future career—and help him keep the peace between his parents.

Walking the L.A. neighborhoods dressed as clowns was not exactly Shia's idea of fun, but it helped make life a little easier for his family. "It always felt safer working . . . from the early days. . . . Every time the makeup would come on, you knew that you were going to have a good time, because they had to sell these hot dogs, and nobody wants to buy a hot dog from fighting clowns," he told Jon Wilde of the *Daily Mail*.

"It was a hustle," he admitted to Dotson Rader, a reporter from *Parade* magazine. "We'd walk around the neighborhood in full clown regalia. My embarrassment factor didn't exist. I had fun, because I knew that in the middle of a performance my parents couldn't fight. So, for sure, every day, there had to be some peaceful time for us, or we weren't going to make it through the week financially."

"It felt safer working . . . because I knew that in the middle of a performance my parents couldn't fight."

The training LaBeouf got from his days out on the sidewalk prepared him for a lifetime of performing in front of others. Fortunately, the older he got, the better the pay. Hot dogs soon gave way to paychecks—and then, to millions.

From a very early age, LaBeouf depended on his cute smile and his charm to get people's attention. In time, these traits would give way to growing talent and experience.

A Rough Start

Shia LaBeouf was born on June 11, 1986, in Los Angeles. He was an only child. His parents were an unusual pair. Father Jeffrey Craig LaBeouf had held a number of jobs, including Cajun circus mime and rodeo clown, and he had even been a member of the road crew for the popular 1970s band the Doobie Brothers. A Vietnam War veteran, he had struggled for years with several kinds of drug addiction. Mother Shayna, on the other hand, was a former ballerina. Dad was 6-foot-4 while Mom was only 4-foot-2. Dad is Cajun, and Mom is Jewish. The two made quite a set of opposites. "They're old hippies," Shia describes to Rebecca Winters Keegan in *Time* magazine.

The LaBeouf family had a difficult time of it, and young Shia had to grow up fast to survive. By the age of ten, he was smoking cigarettes, going to rock concerts with his dad, and gambling in card games. He was kicked out of every school he attended, usually for disruptive behavior. He could not help noticing his parents' constant battle to make ends meet. He found a potential solution at the local beach. As he recalls it, he was watching the waves roll in and out when he made friends with another young man who would come out to surf. That young man was an actor.

"Back in Echo Park, I had a friend I used to surf with and he always had the sickest surfboard and the sickest clothes," Shia said in an interview with *Parade*. "And his mum was always decked out. I used to think, I would love to take my mum shopping and get her all those sorts of clothes. I just knew that money was a solution to whatever . . . was going on in my household. With money, I and my family would have had more options. So I went after a job I thought I could make the most money for a 10-year-old or an 11-year-old boy."

> *"The agent knew I was a kid. . . . Agents are used to parents . . . they're not used to the kid. . . . They liked the fact that I tried."*

The job he came up with, after talking to his friend, was becoming a performer. He began going to local comedy clubs and begging, bribing, and barging his way onto the stage and in front of audiences. People had no idea how to react to this young boy whose act was full of curse words and jokes about adult topics he should not even have known about yet. "My thing was the fifty-year-old mouth on the ten-year-old body," LaBeouf admitted in the same interview. "Sometimes I would bomb. I'd talk about personal stuff and instead of laughing, people would look at me like, 'Oh man, I'm so sorry.' "

Although his act was a hit in many clubs, like the Ice House in Pasadena, it was not enough. He knew that what he really needed was an agent—so he found one. "I went to the Yellow Pages, called up an agent and pretended to be a

In April 2004, LaBeouf appeared at Detail *magazine's "Next Big Thing" celebration. As a young, up-and-coming actor, he was already catching the eye of fans and reporters.*

manager called Howie Blowfish," he told Shannon Harvey in *Perth Now.* "I said I had this great client named Shia, and that he should come in for meetings and auditions. The agent knew I was a kid, but she said she'd never had a kid try to sell himself and that I should come in. . . . Agents are used to parents . . . they're not used to the kid. . . . They liked the fact that I tried."

The agent, Teresa Dahlquist, decided to give him a try and signed him as a client. A decade later, LaBeouf still has the same agent — and jobs are much easier to find.

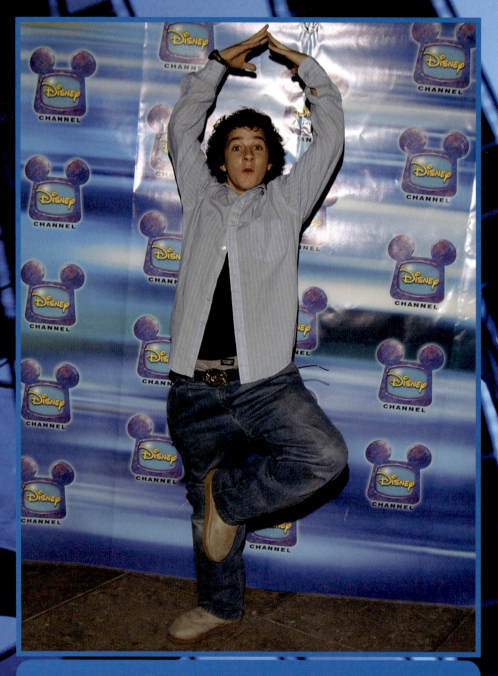

LaBeouf shows off his style and funky sense of humor at the Disney Channel's Children's Television Awards show.

CHAPTER 3

Out on His Own

Dahlquist got right to work looking for acting jobs for this wisecracking, mature teenager. It did not take long to find them. Shia began getting small parts on television series such as *Caroline in the City*, *Touched by an Angel*, *Suddenly Susan*, and *The X-Files*.

In 1999, the Disney network hired Shia to play Louis Stevens on the pilot for a new show called *Even Stevens*. The pilot was a hit, and so was Shia. The series ran for three seasons and created a spin-off movie. It also helped repair a longtime rift between the young actor and his father. LaBeouf's parents had divorced, and by sixteen years old, Shia had moved into his own place. Jeffrey had been in and out of drug rehab centers for years. All of that changed when Shia joined the Disney family. "I was so in love with what I was doing," Shia recalled in an interview with costar John Turturro. "When I got the show, I needed to have a parent on the set, and my mom couldn't do it because she was working at her job. My dad was recovering in a VA [Veterans Administration] hospital at the time. . . . So when he got out, we paid him to come on the set and be with me. . . . That was the beginning of our entire relationship. That show gave me a father and a career and a life."

As time passed and father and son spent more time together, old wounds were healed throughout the family. It also helped keep Jeffrey LaBeouf away from drugs. "We created a rapport. So my acting has helped clean him up, and Mum and Dad are both friends again," he said to reporter Harvey. "So [acting] has given me much more than pride in what I do. It's given me my family back."

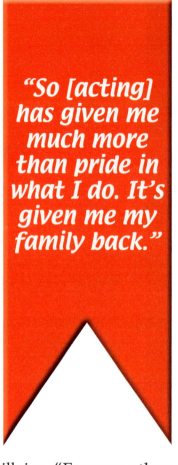

"So [acting] has given me much more than pride in what I do. It's given me my family back."

Even Stevens earned Shia a Daytime Emmy Award—and the attention of movie producers. His first starring role was in the film *Holes*, based on Louis Sachar's Newbery Medal–winning book. In *Holes*, LaBeouf plays Stanley Yelnats, a boy who is shipped off to a shady juvenile detention camp run by treasure-seeking, greedy villains. "Everyone thought I was just a big goofball," LaBeouf explained to Aaron Parsley in *People* magazine. "Holes changed that. When your movie makes almost $70 million, it's a different ball game."

The role also taught him a great deal about the acting business and introduced him to a fellow actor who would become part mentor and part father to him: Jon Voight. "I didn't know anything about this acting business. I never did any training," Shia admitted. "It was all just personality stuff. But when I met Jon Voight on *Holes*, it changed my whole

A sudden success, LaBeouf poses with his Holes *costar, actor and rapper Khleo Thomas. Over the years, Thomas has appeared in a variety of television shows and movies, plus he has released a number of rap songs with artists such as Bow Wow and Soulja Boy Tell 'Em.*

life. He gave me books . . . on acting . . . those books are the only real training I have."

After *Holes*, the movie roles began to come in quicker and quicker. LaBeouf starred in a low-budget true story of golfer Francis Ouimet in *The Greatest Game Ever Played*, then as an intern in supernatural cases in *Constantine* and the voice of Asbel in the English version of *Nausicaä of the Valley of the*

In The Greatest Game Ever Played, *LaBeouf starred as the young golf player who manages to beat his idol in the 1913 U.S. Open. In order to prepare for the role, he practiced two hours a day to learn the sport and improve his swing.*

Wind. In an interview with *The Christian Science Monitor,* producer Ivan Reitman stated that he wanted LaBeouf as soon as he read for *Disturbia.* "He's nice-looking without being too pretty; he's funny and there's an intensity and reality about him that he brings to his roles. Those are the makings of a great movie star," he said.

Reitman was right. LaBeouf's innocent face and easy smile were becoming more and more familiar to moviegoers, but stardom was still waiting in the wings.

Legal Trouble and Stardom

From the very beginning, LaBeouf had to grow up faster than most kids. His childhood went by quickly. He had *1986–2004* tattooed on his wrist to remind him of those years. Becoming an actor only emphasized his need to mature quickly. Even when he was playing characters several years younger than he actually was, he still had to have the discipline, dedication, and determination to play the parts well.

In 2006, he starred in two films that broadened his audience. In *Bobby*, he plays a young man who campaigns for Robert F. Kennedy in 1968 and ends up taking LSD instead of knocking on doors for votes. In *A Guide to Recognizing Your Saints*, he plays a character who has a very strained relationship with his father. The anger he shows in this part is based largely on feelings he has felt in the past about his own father.

That same year, LaBeouf was asked to read for a role in the film *Disturbia*, a modern remake of Alfred Hitchcock's *Rear Window*. When director D.J. Caruso first heard LaBeouf read, he said, "He wasn't attractive. But the more time you spent with him, he became attractive. It happens with his wit, intuition, and timing. Ninety-nine percent of the time, everything he does just happens naturally."

> "It was her first kissing scene too, and I'm drooling all over myself. I looked like a Teenage Mutant Ninja Turtle."

During the filming of *Disturbia*, LaBeouf had one of his first injuries when he had an allergic reaction to medication. When it came time for his first onscreen kiss with costar Sarah Roemer, something went wrong. "I was working out for *Transfomers* all through *Disturbia*," he explained in the *Perth Now* interview, "so my trainer had me taking these amino acid pills. On the bottle he wrote, 'Take a pill twelve times a day.' Who . . . can do that? You won't take twelve of anything a day. So I just took all twelve pills at once." It was not long before his face was tingling, and his lips swelled up like they'd been stung by bees. "By the time I showed up on set, I looked like the Elephant Man." He chuckled. "It was her first kissing scene too, and I'm drooling all over myself. I looked like a Teenage Mutant Ninja Turtle." The scene had to wait until the effects of the medication wore off.

While filming *Disturbia*, LaBeouf was hired to play Sam Witwicky in the mega blockbuster *Transformers*. It was the role that took him from being a very popular actor to being a star. "For me, it's the biggest success that I have ever experienced and I am a very fortunate and blessed human being to be here," he said in a May 2009 interview. "It is the most physically taxing thing that I have ever done in my life

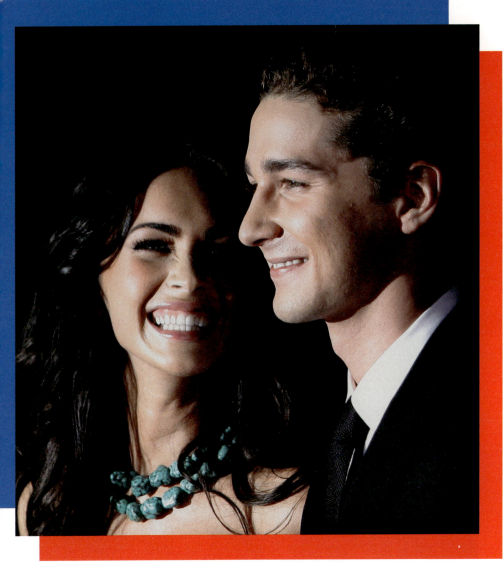

LaBeouf and Megan Fox, his extremely popular costar from the first two Transformers *movies, have become good friends.*

but we are all happy to have jobs, especially with the economy and where the business is at. It is a blessing."

In this movie, LaBeouf's costars ranged from the flesh-and-blood Megan Fox to huge, metallic (and largely computer-generated) Autobots and Decepticons. The movie

The Transformers *movies changed LaBeouf's life. With costars Megan Fox and a troop of gigantic metallic aliens battling to save Earth, Shia became an action hero.*

made millions and put LaBeouf on magazine covers—and in the spotlight.

As he became more popular and his roles (and paychecks) got bigger, LaBeouf also ran into occasional legal trouble. In 1995, he had trouble with the police when he took a knife and threatened a neighbor who had, according to Shia, threatened his mother. In 2007, he was arrested for criminal trespassing when he refused to leave a Chicago drugstore when asked. The charges were dropped. In 2008, he was given a ticket for smoking in a public place—and then got into further trouble when he failed to appear in court for sentencing.

"They had just implemented a law that you couldn't smoke anywhere in Burbank. And I didn't hear about this law, because I was shooting," LaBeouf explained in *GQ*. "The guy gives me a ticket. Then the court date came up two days after I had gotten back from shooting, and I just forgot about it. The news went everywhere, like I was on a crime spree. And it killed me. It broke my heart, because I really try not to be that guy."

He takes full responsibility for his actions, though. "All of the things that have happened in my life have been self-propelled," he said in an interview with *Telegraph* magazine. "I can't blame anybody else or point a finger at anybody."

Like most young people, LaBeouf has made mistakes, but he recognizes them and keeps trying to do better. "What I do know is, I screw up, and I know that I'm working on myself to be a better person," he told Dotson Rader, a reporter for *Parade*. "So I have no apologies. The best I can do is learn from my mistakes and move forward. And that's what I'm trying to do." One step LaBeouf has made is to try to quit smoking. It isn't easy—but not much in his brief life has been.

> "All of the things that have happened in my life have been self-propelled. I can't blame anybody else or point a finger at anybody."

LaBeouf is shadowed by his bodyguard—and friend— Transformer Bumblebee at the 2007 L.A. premiere of the first **Transformers** *movie.*

Starring in Sequels

After *Transformers*, LaBeouf was considered one of the most popular up-and-coming stars of his generation. Steven Spielberg, director of a number of LaBeouf's films, had an explanation. "Shia is within everyone's reach," he told reporter Rebecca Winters Keegan. "He's every mother's son, every father's spitting image, every young kid's best pal and every girl's possible dream. . . . . [DreamWorks] cast him in several bigger-than-life films because we felt those films needed a realistic human anchor."

In 2008 and 2009, LaBeouf made some of the biggest films to hit the screen. He was cast in the fourth installment of the Indiana Jones movies—a job many other actors would have given almost anything to get. LaBeouf recalls the day that Spielberg first asked him about it. As he told Keegan, "Steven said, 'You ever seen *Indiana Jones*?' I said, 'Of course I've seen *Indiana Jones*.' He said, 'Well, we're making another one, and I'd love for you to be in it.' My heart went nuts. I've had anxiety attacks before, but I've never felt that—where you can't breathe and your stomach tenses."

In a 2008 *GQ* interview, costar Harrison Ford stated, "He was unafraid, unabashed. And so straightforward to work with. . . . We never took time out to correct 'acting.' For me, he's the best sort of actor to work with." Spielberg added, "Shia has the appetite and natural ability to play a myriad of characters. I'm not sure what he cannot do."

To get himself physically ready for the intense demands of *Indiana Jones and the Kingdom of the Crystal Skull*, LaBeouf followed a tough exercise program that had him working out three hours a day, seven days a week. "I'll run for an hour and then I'll do two hours of weights," he said. "I have definitely not trained like this for anything in my life. I'm preparing like I'm going into battle." In the film, his character, Mutt Williams, rides a motorcycle, something that LaBeouf enjoys in real life as well. In summer 2009, he put his passion to work for charity when he bought a motorcycle jacket and helmet at a charity auction. He wrote a check for $10,000 to Riders for Health, a group that uses motorcycles to provide health care to African villages.

Along with *Indiana Jones*, LaBeouf also starred in *Transformers: Revenge of the Fallen*. Like the first one, this sequel was a huge blockbuster. He also played Jerry Shaw in *Eagle Eye*, a high-action film that had him running from the FBI, the police—and a computer villain. "There was a CIA agent who was working on the movie with us, and [he] told me . . . [that] one in five phone calls is recorded," LaBeouf told *People* magazine. "[He then] proceeded to play for me a phone call I had made two years prior to signing on to the film. It's pretty terrifying."

Making movies—especially action-packed ones—often involves dangerous stunts. Over the years, LaBeouf has gotten hurt a few times. During *Indiana Jones and the Kingdom of the Crystal Skull*, he injured his rotator cuff (a group of four muscles in the shoulder), as well as some groin muscles. Also, while doing *Revenge of the fallen*, he came very close to

Although LaBeouf and Ford did many of their own stunts in the Indiana Jones movie, they had stunt doubles (above) for the more dangerous ones. Their doubles took the largest risks, and the people in the background were replaced later with time appropriate backgrounds.

receiving a serious eye injury. "We were filming in New Mexico, and it was a chaotic scene," he explained in an interview with *Stumped Magazine.* "I was in the middle of an action scene, winded up impaling my face on a spike. . . . We went to a military hospital and had a guy go like this after he stitched me up [holding finger and thumb and forming a small gap]. I said, 'Oh, what is that?' And he said, '[This far from] blindness.' Yeah, you get beat up doing these things, because that's the way of this movie. It's an aggressive movie; it's an aggressive shoot."

By far, the most serious injury he had experienced by 2009 was a car accident that frightened everyone, including his costar and passenger Isabel Lucas. It also happened while filming *Transformers 2*—though it was not on the set. "I got in a car accident, and my truck flipped three times and landed on my hand," LaBeouf told John Patterson of *The Guardian*. "It was smashed so bad, it didn't look like a hand. . . . To fix this finger, they took bone out of my hip. They'll take more bone to fix another finger." He continued, "I had to pull it [my hand] out from beneath the car. It was either that or wait for the paramedics with the Jaws of Life™ [tools] to arrive and cut it out. I got out, pulled [Isabel] out, walked over to the other car, got them out, and only after doing all that did I realize that I was really messed up."

> "I had to pull it [my hand] out from beneath the car. It was either that or wait for the paramedics with the Jaws of Life . . ."

The seriousness of his accident and the surgeries it has required have been sobering for LaBeouf. "I've been floating on a cloud and this was the first real problem I've had to deal with in a while and it's the first time I've ever dealt with mortality, which is a major thing for a man to deal with in his life," he admitted to *Parade*. "It's a major learning curve and something I'm still dealing with."

Despite the trouble LaBeouf has had in the past, he stays away from drugs, calling his father's lifetime of experience his "personal DARE program." He copes with a great deal of stress in his work but tries to find other ways of handling it.

"The emotional cost is high," he admitted to Patterson. "Your life becomes secondary to your work."

Although rumors are always flying about whom LaBeouf might be dating, he does not go out much. He spends most of his time with friends, family, and English bulldog, Brando. For three years, he was involved with China Brezner, a model and the daughter of producer Larry Brezner. LaBeouf still refers to her as "the love of my life," as he told *Parade* magazine, but he believes it was the pressure of his career that ended the relationship.

LaBeouf has grown close to both of his parents. His father spends half the year living with him and the other half living in a tepee in Montana. His mother lives in a house about ten minutes away from her son, and the two of them are great friends. Shia has been quoted as saying his mother is one of the most wonderful women he has ever known—and the type he wishes he could find for himself one day.

> "I think I grew up a normal kid. . . . I am really proud of my upbringing and I love my folks. I am a happy guy."

When he looks back at his childhood, he sees it positively. "I think I grew up like a normal kid," he told journalist John Hiscock in *Telegraph*. "I just did not go to school like a regular kid, and I had a job and have supported my parents since I was twelve. I am so proud of that. I am really proud of my upbringing and I love my folks. I am a happy guy."

What is next for this young actor? On the horizon were bigger roles in bigger films, including a sequel to the 1987 Academy Award–winning movie *Wall Street* called *Wall*

In the sequel to Wall Street, *LaBeouf wears expensive, tailored suits and carries a leather briefcase. He plays Jacob "Jake" Moore, a young stock trader. It was rumored that he was dating his costar, Carey Mulligan.*

Street: Money Never Sleeps—and yes, *Transformers 3*, which was slated for release in 2011. One thing is sure. Shia LaBeouf will never forget where he came from. "This is just a bigger hot dog that I'm selling," he said in *Time* magazine. "It's the same type of thing. You get dressed up. You do your clown. And if somebody buys a hot dog, then I get Steven Spielberg goin', 'Okay, kid,' instead of my pop now."

CHRONOLOGY

1986	Shia Saide LaBeouf is born in Los Angeles on June 11
1996	Parents split up; enrolls in Thirty-Second Street School, a magnet school for the performing arts
1998	Hires an agent; appears in first television show: *Caroline in the City*
2000–2003	Plays Louis Stevens on *Even Stevens*; wins a Daytime Emmy Award
2003	First leading role in a movie, in *Holes*
2007	Appears in blockbuster *Transformers*
2009	Is injured in a car accident; works with director Oliver Stone in *Wall Street: Money Never Sleeps*
2010	Begins filming *Transformers 3*; is hired for the lead role in 2011's *The Necessary Death of Charlie Countryman*

FILMOGRAPHY

2010	*Wall Street: Money Never Sleeps*	**2004**	*I, Robot*
2009	*Transfomers: Revenge of the Fallen*	**2003**	*The Battle of Shaker Heights*
	New York, I Love You		*Charlie's Angels: Full Throttle*
2008	*Eagle Eye*		*Dumb and Dumberer: When Harry Met Lloyd*
	Indiana Jones and the Kingdom of the Crystal Skull		*Holes*
			The Even Stevens Movie (TV)
2007	*Disturbia*	**2002**	*Tru Confessions (TV)*
	Surf's Up (voice)	**2001**	*Hounded (TV)*
	Transfomers	**2000–2003**	*Even Stevens (TV series)*
2006	*Bobby*	**1998**	*The Christmas Path*
	A Guide to Recognizing Your Saints		*Monkey Business*
2005	*The Greatest Game Ever Played*		*Breakfast with Einstein (TV)*
	Nausicaä of the Valley of the Wind (voice)		
	Constantine		

FURTHER READING

Books

Tieck, Sarah. *Shia LaBeouf*. Pinehurst, NC: Buddy Books, 2008.

Works Consulted

Conley, Kevin. "The (Hot-Dog-Vending, Knife-Fighting, Break-Dancing, Spielberg-Wooing) Adventures of Young Shia LaBeouf." *GQ*, June 2008.
http://www.gq.com/entertainment/celebrities/200805/shia-labeouf-transformers

Harvey, Shannon. "He's a Natural." *Perth Now*, April 14, 2007.
http://www.perthnow.com.au/entertainment/hes-a-natural/story-e6frg3gl-1111113343902

Hiscock, John. "Shia LaBeouf Interview for *Transformers: Revenge of the Fallen*." *Telegraph*, June 11, 2009.
http://www.telegraph.co.uk/culture/film/starsandstories/5506546/Shia-LaBeouf-interview-for-Transformers-Revenge-of-the-Fallen.html

Hogan, Michael. "The New Kid: Landing in Hollywood." *Vanity Fair*, August 2007.
http://www.vanityfair.com/culture/features/2007/08/labeouf200708

Keegan, Rebecca Winters. "The Kid Gets the Picture." *Time*, July 5, 2007.
http://www.time.com/time/magazine/article/0,9171,1640381,00.html

Neumer, Chris. "Shia LaBeouf Interview." *Stumped Magazine,* n.d.
http://stumpedmagazine.com/Interviews/shia-LaBeouf.html

Parsley, Aaron. "Shia LaBeouf: How I'm Getting Buff for *Indiana Jones*." *People*, April 23, 2007.
http://www.people.com/people/article/0,,20036458,00.html

Patterson, John. "I Kiss Trouble." *Guardian*, June 17, 2009.
http://www.guardian.co.uk/film/2009/jun/17/1

Rader, Dotson. "The Mixed-Up Life of Shia LaBeouf." *Parade*, June 14, 2009.
http://www.parade.com/export/sites/default/celebrity/2009/06/shia-labeouf-mixed-up-life.html

FURTHER READING

Randall, Laura. "Shia LaBeouf's Star Gets Brighter." *The Christian Science Monitor*, April 13, 2007.
http://www.csmonitor.com/2007/0413/p15s01-almo.html

"Shia LaBeouf Returns in 'Transformers 2.' " Clickthecity.com, May 28, 2009.
http://www.clickthecity.com/campus/?p=5026

Thomas, Karen. "*Holes* May Mean a Real Opening for Shia LaBeouf." *USA Today*, April 20, 2003.
http://www.usatoday.com/life/2003-04-17-labeouf_x.htm

" 'Transforming' Shia LaBeouf." *Shia LaBeouf Press Archive*, June 25, 2009.
http://www.shialabeouf.us/press/?p=338

Tuturro, John. "Shia LaBeouf." *Interview*, October 2006.
http://justjared.buzznet.com/2006/09/25/shia-labeouf-interview-magazine/

Wilde, Jon. "Why Rising Hollywood Star Shia LaBeouf Will Be the Next Big Thing Since Indiana Jones." *Mail Online*, May 3, 2008.
http://www.dailymail.co.uk/home/moslive/article-563578/Why-rising-Hollywood-star-Shia-LaBeouf-big-thing-Indiana-Jones.html

On the Internet

Hollywood.com: Shia LaBeouf
http://www.hollywood.com/celebrity/1377124/Shia_LaBeouf

Internet Movie Database: Shia LaBeouf
http://www.imdb.com/name/nm0479471/

Shia LaBeouf Fan
http://www.shialabeouf.us/

Shia LaBeouf Online
http://shia-labeouf.biz

PHOTO CREDITS: Cover, p. 27—Barry King/FilmMagic/Getty Images; p. 4—Jeff Vespa/WireImage/Getty Images; p. 6—Gregg DeGuire/WireImage/Getty Images; p. 8—Frederick M. Brown/Getty Images; p. 11—Kevin Winter/Getty Images; p. 12—Amy Graves/Globe Photos, Inc.; p. 15—Lucy Nicholson/Getty Images; p. 16—Supplied by Alpha-Globe Photos; p. 19—AP Photo/Matt Sayles; p. 20—Supplied by ES/Globe Photos, Inc.; p. 22—AP Photo/Mark J. Terrill; p. 25—Bobby Bank/WireImage/Getty Images; p. 28—AP Photo/Charles Sykes. Every effort has been made to locate all copyright holders of material used in this book. If any errors or omissions have occurred, corrections will be made in future editions of this book.